23 Emotions

23 Emotions
by Brittany Leitner

Contents

1. Sonder

The realization that each passerby has a life as vivid and complex as your own.

Those dealing with dying want all of you to shut up.

What do you know about times to pill pop
Or bed pan fried days?

I want to know what it's like to be born into something
I can't get out of

Or what it's like to be the person who says
No such thing; we are all born the same.

For me, living like everyone else meant
Something simple, yellow

Summers, two parents
Maybe a car to get around in

Now I know if we are the same
All we have is waiting

2. Opia

The ambiguous intensity of looking someone in the eye, which can feel simultaneously invasive and vulnerable.

I read somewhere
If we did this long enough
There'd be nothing left to do
But fall in love.
On the days
There's nothing left to do
But fall asleep
I wonder what happened to you

I have to stop telling strangers
What's wrong with me
And falling asleep eyes heavy,
My arms like bricks
Because when I wake up
You're never there

Otherwise, I get along
I'm used to wanting something
And if I wake up all at once
I can't even feel it
What's more pure than waking up
And not remembering?
Instead of sleeping to forget,
You blink to remember

Over and over until it comes
And you're worked back into your earth space
Taking your breath on solid ground

3. Monachopsis

The subtle but persistent feeling of being out of place.

Love is the normal pain
It's the only kind I'll talk about
If I can love, I am like everyone else
It's the part of me my friends know at dinner
When I cry about love
Anyone can sit with me
And not be afraid of me

Love is what dads tell themselves is
Wrong with their daughters
So they don't have to speak to them
It's something that means more to her now
Than it will later
It's the only kind I'll talk about.

4. Énouement

The bittersweetness of having arrived in the future, seeing how things turn out, but not being able to tell your past self.

It's so nice to have a night I did not yet ruin
The one thing I gained with age
Was the ability to stop myself

The only way to have a good fuck
Is to not try to do it again tomorrow

I've never been in love at all
But I'll know him when I feel it

5. Vellichor

The strange wistfulness of used bookshops.

If you think on it too much you'll
never come inside. There are little
shops like this and zones
designated to let out your feelings, so
at work is not the place. If you feel
sad at work it's embarrassing but you
shouldn't go home and feel it either. I think if I could
be okay with feeling everything, none of it would last very long.

I haven't opened in a very long time
I've come a long way from choke holding my
lover and wondering what I can do for money. I was homeless
once, but it feels glamorous because it's
something I can always talk about. You want me to say

I didn't grow up being loved right, but that
isn't true. I grew up loving everything, and I'd like to
think God is a man because the men are not bad.
The men are not bad and you feel bad for them
In the books, and, for the record.

6. Rubatosis

The unsettling awareness of your own heartbeat.

Was I taught my whole life to respond to you?
Laying on your chest, your heart beats faster
It is my cue, my clue that you want me,
My cue to ought to be wanted and to

Fold as I'm told to fold
You can try your best to hold still
But your heart goes off like bath water
The men will not know it's easier to say nothing

My whole world has been waiting for something better
To believe only in the way a girl would believe
And my believing is then pushed toward God and He cries,
He says He never meant to use us like this

7. Kenopsia

The eerie, forlorn atmosphere of a place that is usually bustling with people but is now abandoned and quiet.

I am never happy
Fake it, girl kazoo

8. Mauerbauertraurigkeit

The inexplicable urge to push people away, even close friends who you really like.

Somehow every way I've described
Myself is wrong
In the doorway, you mention we don't
Have much in common
But I have spent hours listening on your father
And your juiced heart, and realize
I have said nothing
I can't think of any other girl suiting you
But I have thought that before and turned up alone
I've gotten too tired to cry so I am too tired for this
And when I cry I hate myself
Remember, he was disgusting
When he pushed into me like that
I trick myself and say it's
Okay for you to come over, fuck me
Just this once – I always believe it
I forget everything that came before this,
Like when you're already in the car home
From somewhere you hated
Why can't I get it right before we end up here?
Before seeing you reminds me of you
Backing up and in again with
My legs shaking for you to do it already
You come out and maybe it's over
Maybe you're thinking of a cigarette, and
Maybe you should have one.

9. Jouska

A hypothetical conversation that you compulsively play out in your head.

Which suit is modest enough?
I need it for a day in the sun with your parents
I just realized there will be no one on my side at my wedding
Your parents may try to see I'm not the one for you
They are wrong; I have to keep quiet about politics
And how I feel about women but just in this instance
Just as they are getting to know me because you already
Know and you listen when I tell you a man shouldn't govern a body
Beach day before wedding day
We are still getting to know each other
Normally I like my boobs pushed up and out but this is my first
One-piece we're all here thankfully they like alcohol and brought it
Alcohol with your parents can't be too drunk drunk enough to stand it
I love you later I love you so much they know we are in love
You touch my side on the sand I'm on the towel you touch me
I am stopped; how can my body go dead when you touch me it must not be
Dead just something it's never felt before it's too much so I think all of me
Stops but really, it is the love kicking in.
Your mother wears a hat I really think I like her I think she will always think
I'm not from the same place as you and I am not
I am from the very bottom I was given nothing I thought it would have to be love
To get me out of the country, the money that comes with love,
But I got myself out
I want this to be your favorite thing about me, maybe it is but your mother will
Never like that about me, she will think too bad when no one is on my side
At our wedding, are you sure she's the one she's never been to Vail she didn't
Grow up going like we did.
But my family, my four-piece, we used to have beach days
And when I was there I never knew I'd be here now, with you, covered up and
Drinking slowly, covered up and so in love in love like I never imagined
Nothing matters except I found it I found
The love and I will wear my plus one proudly and I will get her to like me.

10. Chrysalism

The amniotic tranquility of being indoors in a thunderstorm.

I think I'm not going on enough adventures
Not this, not a glass of wine and a candle
Not alone in The Village   Five years ago
What did it look like to me then?

Why do adventures always involve men?
I once looked someone in the eye and said, "take me out"
It lasted for 4 hours   But then I couldn't get rid of him
When a girl does that, men become obsessed with her

Men, it's the only adventure worth writing home about
We sang karaoke together and then he bought me flowers and then
He fucked   Me
Will he be invited for Christmas?
My mother asks what I did and how I ruined it

11. Vemödalen

The frustration of photographic something amazing when thousands of identical photos already exist.

If it won't change anything,
Why do you do it?
I want to remember this that
It was my eye who saw it
My will that got me here

Is travel for rich folks?
I used to hear my mother
In her number crunch dance,
The way she'd try to give me
Some hope before she said no

I did not have it in me to villainize her
I needed her around to answer
my questions, is travel for the rich folks?
And she never bought a ticket
She never went anywhere

12. Anecdoche

A conversation in which everyone is talking, but nobody is listening

I'm glad my father died before it happened.
I don't know how he would have sat
watching the polls, if he'd be timid or roaring
But I know it'd be at the foot of his bed

silhouette blackened from the light of the flatscreen
snacking on peanuts, choking on peanuts
talking out loud, not even to himself
I remember the day he bought it.

A ceremony ensued with
red blood vessels gathering on his cheeks as
he worked it out of its packaging
It took his whole wingspan to hold it in his arms,

cradle it from the floor to the TV stand
He couldn't see that it looked too big for
his apartment bedroom. He couldn't see
the way I would not touch it.

That's when he tells me he works hard.
He worked hard and this cost
Eight hundred dollars. He hides money
from my mother and you never

think about groceries the same way
once you've seen your father at the checkout line,
telling your mother he only has twenty dollars.
She spends too much, but he needs the big jar of peanuts.

It was at the foot of his bed that he said
he hated Obama and why were there so many
gay people, all of a sudden? It was on the edge
of his bed he cried once and tried to say that he loved me

But by then his words could not reach me
They rolled off of him, falling to his carpet with the peanut shells
and the cardboard box until finally
they settled into something he'd
have to keep stepping on.

13. Ellipsism

A sadness that you'll never be able to know how history will turn out.

I wrote about your death years before it happened
Back then, I wanted to know if I could do this.
I thought of where I'd be, and that
Maybe it wouldn't hurt so bad if I had a lover
To bear with me or if in time
You had realized what you did
Not much has changed,
Now I can say you died out loud in conversation.
It sounds the same as when I say anything,
Only no one ever takes it well.
Your death is a simple fact,
But to me it is yellow drool down your mouth
That I am not disgusted by
It is becoming woman when I wipe it
From you, love
I am woman to feel connected to the nurses,
Kind enough to tell me to get out so they can flip you
Childlike, I think they do that for only me
I fell in love with nurses I had no one to love
Someone tells me to be kind to myself
So I ask him if he'll pray for me
He was just inside me, will he pray for me?
When men speak it's like when the priest spoke
It's like holding your hand, focusing on it
So I don't hear words prayed over you
If I can focus on the squeeze of your hand,
It will be over soon and he will leave.
I don't care who comes and goes,
But I want to remember how your hands look
If I can focus on the squeeze of your hand,
It will be over soon and he will leave.

14. Kuebiko

A state of exhaustion inspired by acts of senseless violence.

I think you can write about killing
Without ever wanting to do it.
I wake up, I remember,
And I want to kill you.

You're standing
At the podium, shouting
Women are murderers, United We Stand
Together, legs spread like banner
Waves. Glittering and reflecting light

And color like cheap replicas,
All printed from the same
Small business in Indiana.
100 copies now for $8.99

At the helm of the crowd,
You say our woman stamp is evil,
You say somewhere up
Inside all of us is the desire
To scoop out life and kill it
Before it gets to taking

To and with this idea,
On your white stage, they
Cheer for you. They were waiting
For this, this act of putting it into words, together
Finally, pinning down our legs, seeing
The ugly and together, it's decided
We need to pay that man in Indiana

15. Lachesism

The desire to be struck by disaster – to survive a plane crash, or to lose everything in a fire.

At the same time, my new love and I
Learned the others would go on without us
And we were like anyone else who paired off
And then
      fell
           off
Like boulders into water
Edged off from the earth

And, then, all at once,
The erotic thought that
Maybe
      we've killed a
             fish

16. Exulansis

The tendency to give up trying to talk about an experience because people are unable to relate to it.

Daddies come to lunch day!
My father sat with me, his legs
Butterflying above the kid's table
Lunchroom: Turkey Chip
sandwich pressed cold no cheese
lumpy sharp meat, crunch
Learning what "done!" means

Whole dodge of hunger
What's the meal you ate
When you thought no one could die?
I did not know there'd be a day
I'd stop loving him
I should have known;
He was messing me up:
Chips are the side to the sandwich
The intermission, the back and forth
The lesson: "You can't have everything at once"

Dad did this wrong. Wait.
The patience, the slow build of love
I'm taught to look for in men after you
I had to have you all at once
At lunch —
Turkey Chip with my father

I, extension of him,
Tall as his knee,
My father, my olly olly oxen free

17. Adronitis

Frustration with how long it takes to get to know someone.

In the bar, after two frozen painkillers
He asks what I never told anyone, if I could tell him.
In my childhood mind, this was my moment.
I have a boy who's asking about me, who could love me
At least enough to not be turned off by what I have to say next
In the room with my twin bed and magazine clipped walls
I imagined escape in the shape of being loved
And love meant I could spill my secrets

So why can't I say it now? Why was homelessness suddenly
Something that never happened to me? Why is a dead father
Something that happened in a movie I saw?
I took it and took it, and now
I decide if I'll take it from you.

18. Rückkehrunruhe

*The feeling of returning home after an immersive trip only to find it fading
rapidly from your awareness.*

In the morning, in our foreign bed
I look over and realize how much I've
Missed you. You spent the day away from me
Sick, rocking, sleeping through the sun as
I found ways to busy myself and pretend
I was enjoying vacation.

The only part of this trip I liked
Was having someone to fly with,
You telling the attendant we were
Together when she tried to move us
Me lifting up the armrest that divides us
Holding your arm and folding over your knee
Until I was taking up all of what was
Supposed to be your side.

19. Nodus Tollens

The realization that the plot of your life doesn't make sense to you anymore.

In the days that followed
She was expected to get better
I've been in rooms like these with
A mix of sour light and sun
A rival to her cocktail shot in the arm,
That's supposed to put the life in

I knew she would live
It's the men who were always dying
Picture this: last movie you saw, the
Family crying together
Talking about what they miss...
Isn't it always a father?

I know not everything means
Something, but what can be said of
The men who are dying? I can't look at
Them, the way they demand our worlds
Knowing they'll leave first
And leave me to carry on, to be free

I can't look at them and I'm not
Looking at her. Women cannot even
Have this, the expectation to die,
The moment to revel in the worry of those
Around her, the one hour in the night to smile
To think, what we all might all do without her.

20. Onism

The frustration of being stuck in just one body, that inhabits only one place at a time.

Of course I've always been fascinated
With how men find their way around us
I make love to you and try to find
A way to tell you this is all new to me
But I am not ashamed that my first lovers
Have already been taken and went through or
That I couldn't bear to look them in the eye
Or have clear eyes when I bore them
How else would I know to love you know?
How would I know to be sure of you when you nod,
And know what I mean when I say it's my first time.
I wake you up to draw it out of you
Spit on the sprinkler of creamy love

21. Liberosis

The desire to care less about things.

he holds my head in his hands and
he doesn't call me a mexican. i think, su madre
would approve; there's a word for brown mothers and
what they think is best: blanqueamiento. it took a while
to know the word for it, that brown mothers are similar if
not the same, and even i, third generation texas america, was
not excluded from that. i am tall and thin,
not like a mexican, and he looks to me when trying to think
of a spanish word; he does not forget.
would you have let men take photos of you naked so you could
pass through america and put on your hoop earrings
and pretend nothing happened to you?
that's the most american thing in the world: to pretend
do i love him because my mother said I should, or do
i love him? mi abuelita tells stories of brown women
trying to pass to america and pass with a chemical bath
because americans didn't know what brown would do to them,
they didn't know if brown would stick, if la tos was different
if brown was contagious. my grandma was not yet born when she
came in and there were stories of women being photographed.
brown nipples eyeing down the polaroid arms up over
their heads to pass through. some say they hung in bars,
on desk tables, and she doesn't know
if her mother was one of them.

22. Altschmerz

Weariness with the same old issues that you've always had – the same boring
flaws and anxieties that you've been gnawing on for years.

On the menu today is the
Idea that love will kill me
Not like an offing, all at once,
But a what's next moment, fade into nothing
The way my father faded out
Of his life years before his body
Did the killing for him

In this room, in our state, it is
Her job to crack me
She sits across from me to set up her power
Her lone chair to my three-some couch, built
Somewhere for entertaining. The extra space so I don't fall off
And end up somewhere else
She taps a little at first and asks me

Where I feel it. When I close my eyes, it hurts everywhere,
But I tell her it's in my chest and we start there.
Now, it is my job to remember
In my bedroom with my father screaming
At me from the other side, I dreamt of love
As I sat behind my door on the ground against it,
Love oozed down around me

And it did the job of keeping him out.
It dripped from the ceiling down the
Space that connected him to me in the
Same breath, same gene pool
Love will set you free,
And as I remember those words, those thoughts,
That fear, she asks what's coming up for me.

My eyes are still closed but now I'm in a cold
Cement room, and I won't let the light in
I'm in this room without love but it's fun

To think maybe it's on the other side somewhere.
I'm thinking she'll want to smash the walls or
Have some sort of smashing-of-walls moment,
But instead, she ask me what the wall is doing.

I say it's keeping me from love and I cannot
See beyond it. Beyond the walls I die
Happiness was getting out of bedroom
And going to find love, but
I'm out of room, and with cement,
And if I get out, there's nothing left,
I didn't know ultimately, this was what I thought

Of love, of finding the thing I spent so many days
Ringing my eyes over, asking for it
Each year with a side of birthday cake.
She says, "for you, love is annihilation" and she asks
Me to talk to the walls. I stand in the room and inch
By each cinder block I run my fingers
Over the lines until I've touched every edge.

She asks again, where do I feel it?
It's everywhere, there is no light
I'm boxed in, I cannot see beyond it
She says stand in the center of the room and don't move.
She asks where I feel it
And at the end, as if we were two polite strangers,
She asks me to close my eyes and she asks me to thank it

To see if I can thank it.

23. Occhiolism

The awareness of the smallness of your perspective.

I hardly even notice hurricanes anymore
When I stopped feeling sad I was shocked
the way some people are shocked when

something bad happens.
Of course, I prefer strangers.
They're always smiling and saying
whatever the most important thing is
first.

Brittany Leitner is a poet and journalist living in New York City. She's the winner of the International Merit Award in poetry from the *Atlanta Review*, and has been published in *Time Out New York* and Elite Daily. She can be reached on social media @britariail.

Made in the USA
Lexington, KY
22 November 2019